TRANSFORMING CLAY INTO VESSELS OF HONOR

– MINISTRY FOR THE HEART!

By Maria Rice

Copyright © 2006 by Maria Rice

Transforming Clay into Vessels of Honor
by Maria Rice

Printed in the United States of America

ISBN 1-60034-235-3

All rights reserved solely by the author. The author guarantees all contents are original and do not infringe upon the legal rights of any other person or work. No part of this book may be reproduced in any form without the permission of the author. The views expressed in this book are not necessarily those of the publisher.

Unless otherwise indicated, Bible quotations are taken from The Full Life Study Bible-King James Version. Copyright © 1992 by Life Publisher's International.

www.xulonpress.com

Dedication:
For those who encouraged me
along the way to never give up, I thank you

TABLE OF CONTENTS

Prayer ix

Introduction xi

Lesson 1   Dare to be different –
           Whose life are you living? 15

Lesson 2   Dare to have a God confidence -
           What is your hope built upon? 21

Lesson 3   Dare to be released –
           Changing of the Guard. 33

Lesson 4   Dare to be invisible –
           Can you see ME? 47

Lesson 5	Dare to be broken – Let's get ready to H-U-M-B-L-E!	59
Lesson 6	Dare to be consumed – Beautiful for Ashes.	73
Lesson 7	Dare to climb aboard - He is the Potter and we are the clay.	85
Lesson 8	Dare to be a Vessel of Honor – Fit for the Master's use	97

Conclusion 105

Closing Prayer 109

ACKNOWLEDGEMENTS / REFERENCES / BIBLIOGRAPHY... 113,115,117

Let us pray

Gracious Lord, You are so wonderful and magnificent. The closer you draw us to you the more we are reminded of our own limitations.

So, Dear Lord, it is our hearts' desire to be more like you. We invite you to represent yourself through us. We yield up our lives, arms, hands, legs, minds, and hearts along with ever endeavor to you for inspection. Search us and know us and change us into reflections of your grace.

Father God, as you transform us into the image of your precious son, remind us that our light affliction is but for a little while working for a more excellent and eternal glory. Remain near to us while you work on us, in us and through us.

For the work that you do through us, we will be mindful to give you all the glory, all the praise and all the honor. We realize that it was not of our power or might but by your spirit, Dear Lord.

Transforming Clay into Vessels of Honor

Lord God, it is with a humble heart that we pray in the mighty matchless name of your Son, Jesus.

Amen

Introduction

Are you feeling a gentle nudge? Maybe it's a push? How about fire under your feet? Have you grown curious of learning new things all of a sudden? Have you grown uncomfortable with television, radio, old hangouts and old friends? Are you growing weary of the turmoil today? How about frustrated with the daily gossip at the water fountain? Or what about the dis-ease you feel when you remember that you should have prayed for a dear friend in distress, but didn't? If so, you are experiencing the many ways God calls us to change. Perhaps it is a major life overhaul or an impulse to better manage your family, time, emotions, and money.

This book is written out of my calling to assist others to mature, to grow and to become all that they can be as kingdom heirs. It is written to assist you during your personal transformation while you are being formed, defined and refined into

Vessels of Honor. There are several biblical passages referring to vessels, as the material they are composed of, their function, even the processes of make them. I have sometimes wondered if the composition determined its function, or if the function determined the composition materials.

I encourage you to read this book slowly. Pause frequently and ask the Holy Spirit to teach you. Meditate on your life as it was, is and will be. God speaks to us in many different ways. I encourage you to write them into a journal as you undergo this change process. Reflection will come naturally, and sometimes it is even painful to see the real us. During these times, stay focused on Jesus and be assured that you are the beloved of Christ. You may have mixed feelings about the things you will see in yourself, but remember, Jesus said, he wouldn't leave you comfortless.

The idea of being without comfort is distressful to say the least. While fear of the unknown has enough power to cripple a life, sometimes leaving us mentally, physically, emotionally and even spiritually retarded. When considering the changes you have encountered, endured and overcome in your life thus far, reflect on the strength it took to make it through. It took pure, raw, unadulterated courage to come out on the other side of every midnight, crawl out of each valley and to scale the perilous cliffs to reach the mountaintop.

Yet for others, it is the fear of remaining the same, veiled in consistency, with potential never energized that inspires their growth. This fear can become a burden while they seek to satisfy their desires which propel them to lunge forward into a world of mysterious delights and hidden treasures of self-awareness, if they move outside of God's will for them.

Yet we are still finding ourselves unfulfilled and with more questions to answer than ever before. What will satisfy our thirst and hunger? What will cool our burning desires of knowing who we are and what we were created to be? This book will help you discover just what it means to be a new creation, having put off the old man and aid you in the putting on Christ! Also if you are a mature Christian, this book will add some seasoning to your salt!

Finally, be encouraged to celebrate your transformation for you are fearfully and wonderfully made. Each stage of life is an open window into the spiritual realm where we are designed for a specific mission to fulfill and to gain instructions for the next. God has, is and will continue to design us for each moment we live as He also designs the moments we live for us. So celebrate because as long as you are alive and have a relationship with the Living God, you will forever more be in the best time of your life!

Whose life are you living?

"Teach me to do thy will, for thou art my God; thy spirit is good; lead me into the land of righteousness."
Psalm 143:10

<u>Dare to be different!</u>

"And be ye not conformed to this world: but be ye transformed by the renewing of your mind, that ye may prove what is that good, and acceptable and perfect will of God."
Romans 12:2

We've all seen them, those people who are just a little different. We find ourselves wondering what makes her or him different from everyone else. We know snippets of their lives. They endure woes, hardships and troubles yet, they have an uncanny peace about them. What is it that makes them different?

These are people we want to get to know. We desire a private session with them to ask them, "What is it about you"? We feel drawn to them, and they always receive us openly. And they will always turn to us and explain the reason for their hope, peace and joy. They have fallen in love with someone who has worked inside them to give them these precious gifts.

When we commit ourselves to God and his will, anything can happen. We find ourselves saying and doing things we'd never imagined. We observe God working in miraculous ways. We participate in the redemption of his people. We feel joy. We marvel at the Lord.

I know that's what happened to me. One day, I laid down my will and took up His. Living in a chaotic time, I sought for something more. I'm sure you've been there too. Wondering how you are going to pay the bills, feed the children, run errands, even extending selfless acts of kindness, only to discover at the end of the day, that we are still empty, shallow and wanting.

Turning to the book of Judges, I read a story about a woman named Deborah. She was a prophetess and warrior. Her story was so not like my own. But I was drawn to her because of her trust in the Lord, and the faith of the people for her. But what does her story have to do with us? Most of us won't be prophets, judges, or leaders of nations. In fact, we feel ordinary and unnoticed most of the time. What we forget is that following God makes us different – from unbelievers, but also from one another. God has created each of us uniquely and for a specific purpose. And in that purpose we can dare to accomplish what he asks of us.

When we allow ourselves to be set apart for God's use, we will find ourselves leading in one way or another. Perhaps not as presidents or judges (though some of us will!), but certainly as mothers, managers, employees, performers, professionals, business owners, ministry directors, intercessors, Sunday school teachers, community volunteers and more. Whatever our God-endowed roles in life, being separated unto the Lord distinguishes us as people of faith and influence.

The next time you open your bible, notice all the people who dared to live for Him and were set apart for God's will. In fact, I dare you to try step out of the norm. Dare to differ from the normal roles for men and women in our culture; different in values from our society stamps on us; even being different in the way you handle your successes and failures. Remember that the most important part of being different, is committing your life to the Lord God.

How does someone become living for God – and make a difference – for God? Author and theologian C.S. Lewis explained it this way:

"The Christian way is different: harder, and easier. Christ says "Give me ALL. I don't want so much of your time or so much of your money and so much of your work: I want YOU. I have not come to torment your natural self, but to kill it. No half-measures are any good. I don't want to cut off a branch here and a branch there, I want to have the whole tree down. Hand over the whole natural self, all

the desires which you think innocent as well as the one you think wicked – the whole outfit. I will give you a new self in its stead. In fact, I will give you Myself; my own will shall become yours."

For this lesson of Transformation we dare to live for God. The following questions will help us with our journey.

- To you, what does it mean to be different for God in your daily life?

- How do you feel about C.S. Lewis's definition of the Christian way of being different? What would be hard about it? What would be easy?

- If you dare to live for God, how might your life change?

- How would you like to make a difference for him?

- Living for God means....

- How can you distinguish between "being different by living for God" and just plain rebellion? For example, if you decide to "go against the crowd," how do you know whether you're following God's desire or your own?

- In our culture, what challenges face a person who dares to live for God? How can you overcome these challenges?

- What could be the benefits of living for God?

- What key points did you learn in this lesson?

- How will you work them into your life?

- How will you teach others?

A Challenging prayer!!!!

Dear Lord,

I am no longer my own, but Yours. Put me in what You will, rank me with whom You will: Put me to doing: put me to suffering: Let me be employed for You, or laid aside for You: Exalted for You, or brought low for You; Let me be full, let me be empty: Let me have all things: let me have nothing: I freely and heartily yield all things that I am and will be for Your pleasure and disposal. And now, gracious and blessed God, Father, Son and Holy Spirit, You are mine and I am Yours. So be it. AMEN.

My hope is built on (?????)

"Now FAITH is the substance of things hoped for, the evidence of things not seen." Hebrews 11:1

Dare to have God-confidence

"And be ye not conformed to this world: but be ye transformed by the renewing of your mind, that ye may prove what is that good, and acceptable and perfect will of God." Romans 12:2

As we move forward toward our life giving, life changing heavenly Father, at some point, we shed the disillusion of ourselves and become aware of His awesome greatness. It's impossible to draw near a holy God and not become aware of our unholiness. But as we spend time with Him our hearts will begin to change and we will start to become aware that it most certainly is ALL ABOUT HIM.

Approaching the Lover of our souls, we fall headlong in love with him. Or at least I pray that you do. Seek intimacy with him. Steal away, to be with him. By choosing to be intimate with our Lord and Savior our lives change. Yes, really!

I imagine it to be like braiding three cords together. And according to Ecc. 4:12 a threefold cord is not easily broken. The more intimate we become the stronger the connection will be. To remain carnally minded and a flesh feeder would weaken the connection. That's because true intimacy doesn't begin in our flesh. True intimacy just like true love, true affection, and true passion begins far away on a spiritual plane. Where and how? Good questions! It begins with two five-letter words: FAITH and TRUST.

Surprisingly, faith and trust go hand in hand. Each feeds upon the other, just like each breeds upon the other. The more trust I have the deeper my faith. The deeper my faith the higher my trust. Look at it this way...

Picture a tree: Faith is the root (the substance of things hoped for / the work-horses) and trust is the branches and leaves (evidence of things unseen). In other words the things that are going on in the root produces the healthy or mutated crop!

Faith manifest trust by providing life-giving nutrients from the soil (by what we feed into our minds and digest into our hearts) along with WATER (the word of God – life giving waters; which shower blessings grace, promises, anointing, judgment down and pour it upon us) which is the medium to flow through the truck, branches and leaves. Faith spreads abroad to support the weight of the trust.

Trust manifest faith by absorbing and converting protons (light – God's love, mercy, grace, glory; which dispels darkness Col. 1:13) into the leaves and breaking it down through photosynthesis (trials, tests, temptations, and tribulations) to simple sugars (compassion / gentleness / temperance). The more light the leaves capture the more sweetness is produced. So, with that knowledge intimacy blossoms into fruit, the sweeter it will be. That fruit is genuine, true, pure, affectionate, passion of love; which is expressed as the fruit of the spirit... Love, joy, peace, goodness, gentleness, temperance, patience, faith and meekness.

So each piece of fruit contains seeds to perpetuate intimacy, more faith and trust. Basically, this illustration says that we can continue to connect spiritually or we can destroy what God's spirit has so carefully put together.

How do we destroy God's image from being reflected in our lives? How do we get to the point of limiting His glory in us? How do we, earthen vessels change from being vessels of honor to vessels of dishonor? Our fruit is demished by the pestilences of doubt, fears, insecurities, and distance from the Father. For this reason, Jesus said in John 15:1-8, I am the true Vine, and my Father is the vinedresser. Every branch in Me that does not bear fruit He takes away; and every branch that bears fruit He prunes, that it may bear more fruit. You are already clean because of the word which I have spoken to you. Abide in me, and I in you. As the branch cannot bear fruit of itself, unless it abides in the vine, neither can you, unless you abide in me. I am the vine, you are the branches. He who abides in me, and I in him, bears much fruit; for without me you can do nothing. If anyone does not abide in me, he is cast out as a branch and is withered and they gather them and throw them into the fire and they are burned. If you abide in me and my words abide in you, you will ask what you desire, and it shall be done for you. By this my Father is glorified, that you bear much fruit, so that you will be my disciples. This pestilence becomes blight to the tree of intimacy, causing pain, destruction and eventually death.

Ever notice how painful it is to not have faith? Or how destructive it is to distrust? Both breed death.

So what does this confident intimacy look like? We, who are Christ's disciples approach and develop relationships which have our precious Lord as its root. We are more giving, patient, and loving. We have no fear of hurts and wounds, because we are dispensing his love through us.

Each relationship which does not have Him as its center will be reduced to focusing on themselves and will result in doomed. For instance, as long as I focus on you and you focus on me, we will not grow close together. I will know understand you, nor will you understand me. However, once I change my focus from you and move closer to God, He will bring me closer to you, teaching me how to minister to your needs. We are not thrown together by accident. Each relationship is a perfect plan of Father. The diagram below illustrates how each relationship bond is formed and glorifies our Father.

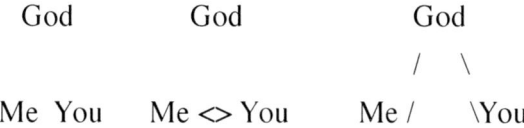

Each relationship which doesn't focus on God will not ascend. No bond will form the valley will remain equidistant no matter how close we appear. But when the focus shifts to God, then the two ascend and move closer to one another.

Peter, also gives us great insight on relationship and a godly confidence. In 2 Peter 1, he explains where the source of our confidence comes from and how it is to be dispensed. Verses 2-11 is our maturity chart. It's what we use to evaluate our faith and trust in our Lord.

It reads, "Grace and peace be multiplied to you in the knowledge of God and of Jesus our Lord, as His divine power has given to us all things that pertain to life and godliness, through the knowledge of Him who called us by glory and virtue, by which have been given to us exceedingly great and precious promises, that through these you may be partakers of the divine nature, having escaped the corruption that is in the world through lusts. But also for this very reason given all diligence, add to your faith (hope in the promises) virtue (power to endure); and to virtue knowledge(the confidence and assurance); and to knowledge temperance(flexiblility and maliable); and to temperance patience(endurance); and to patience godliness(which is the manifestation of holiness in the situation - radical holiness); and to godliness brotherly kindness (compassion for others and self-sacrifice) and to brotherly kindness charity (LOVE). *For if these things are yours and abound, you will be neither barren nor unfruitful in the knowledge of our Lord Jesus Christ. For he who lacks these things is shortsighted, even to blindness, and has forgotten that he was cleansed from his old sins. Therefore, brethren, be even more diligent to make your call and election sure, for if you do these things you will never stumble; for so an entrance will be supplied to you abundantly into the everlasting kingdom of our Lord and Savior Jesus Christ.*

- *Have you ever taken God at his word*. You can, he's trustworthy. He proclaimed his word to be above even his name. Think about that for a moment. He has fidelity with his word.
- *Are you willing to go against the crowd*. He promised that when we turn toward Him, that He will be there for us. He will be our comfort, our strength, our refuge and not put us to shame. And he that promised, is faithful. How about us? Do we have enough faith to go against the crowd? In my case, God has called me to go against the crowd at the lunch table with my friends. The hour was spent in much gossip against other coworkers. Even though when I announced that I would no longer be a party to gossip, many at the table were trying to coax me back in. Finally, I had to take a stand and changed my lunch time or

sit at another table. It was a critical decision, I know however that I must obey God rather than men and women.

How about you? Can you think of even one area in your life where you are going against the crowd? If not, perhaps you are being conformed to this world, rather than being transformed by the renewing of your mind. (Romans 12:2).

- *We have examples all throughout scriptures of people who believed God and their lives reflected it.* Each one's faith was translated into tangible action: Noah built an ark; Abraham left home; Jacob returned home; Joseph's faith elevated him to be in a position to help others; Joshua and Caleb had the confidence that God could and would do anything for his beloved; Rahab hid spies and helped them escape; Esther, Daniel, Nehemiah, Josiah, John the Baptist, Paul, Peter (yes, even Peter). These are just a few examples, there are far too many to name here. But each one mentioned in the scriptures of those who lived in the confidence of our God. Our greatest example is found in the life, death, resurrection of our Lord and Savior, Jesus Christ, the Son of the Living God. He lived, breathed and exemplified godly confidence for us to look upon; Even to the point of laying their life on the line. He believed God, that's why he was willing to do whatever he could to further God's agenda. That's how He became a vessel God could use.

How does your faith translate into tangible action? Again, can you think of one specific action you've taken in response to believing God?

- *Do you trusted God to take care of you?* Have you ever entrusted your life into the hands of your enemies, knowing that the Lord would take care of you?

Is there anything in your life that gives you evidence you are counting on God, and God alone, to take care of you? Or do you constantly hedge your bets, setting up a contingency plan, just in case God doesn't come through?

So many people have taken God at his Word and are willing to go against the crowd. Each one believed God and did something about it. Even in the midst of their circumstances, they believed that God would take care of them, and refused to waste time developing a contingency plan. Do you see the benefits of having a total God-confidence. Do you? If we want to be remembered as men and women of faith, we would do well to follow in the footsteps of our examples in scriptures, a godly friend who exhibits this confidence would be our role model.

For this lesson of Transformation: developing a God-confidence and why that might seem peculiar to the world. The following questions will help us with our journey.

- Name four reasons why our examples in scripture is a model of faith for you?

- Do you have this same confidence in God?

- Do you take God at his Word? Do you believe he will do what he said he will do? How does your life show evidence of that belief?

- Are you willing to go against the crowd if God calls you to? Give specific examples of something you've chosen to do, which involved/involves going against the crowd.

- Does your faith translate into action? How?

- Do you believe God will take care of you? Or do you try to escape difficult situations on your own or at least have a contingency plan? Again, give a specific example of an area in your life where you are completely dependent on God to take care of you.

- Do you know that Jesus is praying that your faith will not fail?

- What key lesson did you glean from this study?

- How will you display your hope in God in your own life?

- How will you encourage others to put their hope in God?

Our Prayer

Father God, we come before your throne of grace to first acknowledge that you are God above all. We have read in your word, that without faith it is impossible to please you. Lord God we freely ask you to increase our faith and to strengthen up our faith in areas still lacking while we are learning to have more confidence in you. Father we thank you for your Son, who had confidence in you that you could and would do anything to bring us back to yourself. His confidence inspires us and encourages us to step out and deepen our trust and faith in you.

Father God, we grant you to look into our hearts and to shine your precious light to expose those areas to us. But we will not just look upon them but we freely grant you access to test our faith as well. We also ask you to strengthen us during our time of testing, Father. O God, we thank you that you would allow us to be renewed day by day and to be transformed into the perfect image of your son, Jesus. For this we give you praise, glory and honor. In Jesus name we humbly pray. AMEN.

Changing of the guard!

"Search me, O God and know my heart: try me, and know my thoughts: and see if there is any wicked way in me, and lead me in the way of everlasting."
Psalm 139:23-24

Dare to Release!

"And be ye not conformed to this world: but be ye transformed by the renewing of your mind, that ye may prove what is that good, and acceptable and perfect will of God."
Romans 12:2

Read Psalm 139 (in entirety)

In the world we are expected to acquire more and more. Catch phrases like, bigger, better, new and improved floods our marketplaces edging us to keep up with the Jones'. Someone even came up with a slogan; "He who dies with the most toys, wins". This has always left me perplexed. It always left me wanted to know, what would I really win if I gain the whole world and all that she has to offer?

In contrast, we who are saved, we are asked to give up, give away, release and discount. We're asked to release hopes, dreams, goals, our children, our very lives in a society where "more is better". The more allowances we make for the Lord to transform us, the more we are required to release. For some of us, it might be to become better stewards of our finances, time, families, or the words that we speak. When we hurt badly enough, we gladly go to God to ask him to remove the source of our pain. Sometimes we are shocked to find out that the very source is us, ourselves. This is why we have difficulty when he tells us that we are in need of an attitude adjustment and a changing of the guard.

In our reading the psalm starts and concludes with two striking verses: "search me and known me" and "search me, try me and know my thoughts: and see if there is any wicked way in me, and lead me in the way everlasting." Wow, isn't that a heartfelt statement? God already knows everything about us, and yet, we don't see ourselves as he does. David asks the hardest question of God in this scripture, he asked for exposure of himself to himself. He asks to be moved from his negativity and character flaws traits.

Removal doesn't come easy for us in the areas where we think we have it all together. It doesn't come natural to us to submit our giftings, talents, knowledge and skills to him. Why, because we have learned that they produce success or acknowledgement in us and for us. But, he desires the whole loaf not just a couple slices of bread. He desires our whole being to be used for his purposes. In this chapter we will explore, submission to God and what it looks like and the results it produces.

While total submission doesn't always feel good, but it will produce peace within our spirits. So, while we are being poked and prodded on our Master potter's wheel, be comforted with this truth: as we commit our ways to the Lord and acknowledge him in all of our way, leaning not to our own understanding, he will (not sometimes will, but always will) direct our path. And He is leading me where, is the question all the control personalities types are asking, right? He is leading us into his will, his way, his truth and toward Christ likeness. So what does submission look like? I am reminded of the Tomb of the Unknown Solider to be a key example to explain submission.

No trip to the capital of our nation would be complete without a visit to the Arlington National Cemetery. While the eternal flame at Kennedy's grave and the volume of white crosses as grave markers are captivating, you must see the changing of the guard at the tomb of the unknown solider. What an impressive sight for adult and child to witness. The tomb is a symbol and men and women who lost there lives in battle during World War One. A solider is posted guard and patrols this tomb. As he paces back and forth in front of the tomb holding an M-16 rifle, the magnitude of awe comes to my mind.

These soldiers work in shifts. When one shift is over, another guard comes to the paddock, and an officer oversees the exchange. They salute and do really slick moves with their rifles; they pass each other, salute, spin their weapons and toss them in the air. Again, it is really quite impressive to behold. All this takes place under the watchful eyes of civilian and military witnesses. This also occurs without rebuttal, or complaining or muttering from the dead solider!

We, who are born-again, undergo a similar experience. Even more so with us, during our new birth experience through maturity, we have posted guards from the Host of Heaven to watch over us. We are told in the Paul's letter to the Philippians that "the peace of God, which passes all understanding, shall keep your hearts and minds through Christ Jesus. Furthermore, we know that this guard of peace was ordained of God in Isaiah 26:12. Just like in a military regiment, they have their orders.

As we mature (transform) in Christ, we realize we are soldiers engaged in a battle that started before time began. We are in battles and under siege for our very souls and for the souls we were saved to reach. Each battle will be fought to remove a stronghold. A stronghold is a heavily manned and fortified fortress with high thick walls. While this is a natural description, spiritually, we have erected strongholds with the bricks and mortar of our hurts, fears, anxieties and passions. Our ancestors erected some that we continue to maintain today.

This is why we see repeated patterns of unforgiveness, self-hatred, anger, alcoholism, deviant behaviors, divorces, abuse, deceit, and every kind of perversion, addictive behaviors, and the inability to finish started projects as well as other disorders running rampant through our family lineage. We lug and carry our self-made fortresses with us when we come to Christ. Yet when we are born again and during our transformation we need our hands free for the battlefield.

Some wars are fought and won easily yet others last for years. Why, you ask? Jesus answers – some only come out by prayer and fasting – we must bind the strong man before we can enter into his house and spoil his goods.

Demolitions of some fortresses which fall immediately are much like the battle of Jericho. To illustrate the walls tumbled when the children of Israel marched in silence for seven days around the fortified city. And on the seventh day they marched seven times around the fortified city. Then they raised their voices in a shout to the Lord.

While during our re-birth we are told that all the angels of heaven rejoiced. I've never experienced a group who rejoiced silently. It's always a loud clamor! When they are reborn, some plagues were immediately removed by the rejoicing of the saints, angels and the saved. These plagues were never again to be revisited, the stronghold was broken!

Now that we are born again and being transformed into the image of Christ, we must allow Christ-likeness to be our main objective. Jesus said that of the great works he did, we can do also and more. Well if He kicked the devil's butt so can we. But first, we must prepare ourselves to be in the will of God for every battle. We forget that the battle is the Lord and he promised that he will fight for us. Read Ex. 14:14,

Duet. 1:30, 1:42, 3:22, 20:4 and 2 Ch. 20:17 for proof. We must adjust our attitude to know when to stand and when to stand down.

Second, we must understand three separate but conjoined passages. In Ephesians, we must be strong in the Lord and in the power of his might. Too many of us are fighting battles that we are not empowered to win. Too many of us are spiritually whipped and can't figure out why? The walking wounded and war battered saints of the kingdom of God is not a good witness to your fellow believers and to the unsaved. Mortified they witness that the battle is too great and are weary. Too often, the saints compromise the glory of eternity because the price of submission was too great. However, the mark of the champion is to know when to pause, be still, and to stand and when to strike!

It is a tragedy to see the saints not prepared, not knowing the wiles of their enemy for they become the walking wounded perplexed in distress. It is also a trick of the enemy. To get us to fight for things that don't belong to us (if God asked for it if you keep it – you have to fight to maintain it). We sometimes fight with demons whose assignment was long past due, but we hold on to the treasured memory for the sheer drama of it all. We become attention seeking, ministry grabbing, prophesy snatching junkies. We fight in arenas where we have no claim or authority. All we are required to do is, be strong in the Lord – not by power or by might, but by my spirit says the Lord.

Next, we are leaving home half dressed. We are not prayed up and girded up in the word enough to fight. Yet, we go on the battle field and get whooped and are surprised. We are instructed to put on the whole armor of Christ. So why are we leaving home naked? Really, that's what we look like when we are only partially spiritually dressed. We are instructed to put on the whole armor then we can stand against the wiles of the enemy and standing victoriously and behold the salvation of the Lord.

Third, we must know how to weld the weapons we have. Knowing that they are not carnal then we must also acknowledge that the battle isn't carnal either. Have we forgotten so quickly the power of praise, prayer, fasting, worship, and devotion? Have we forgotten the power of mercy, grace and forgiveness? These weapons are not created in the world so they will not be comfortable using them against the world. Too quickly we desire to return evil for evil. But, holding our peace is a weapon.

We also have the power and authority to use the name of Jesus, draw a bloodline and remind the enemy that he can't come any further and to use the word of God as a two-edge sword to slice and dice between soul and spirit. Intriguing! Why would we allow our soul-man to hold onto our hurts, wounds, and lusts, the word of God is able to separate it from us.

The scripture is quiet clear on the power of the name of Jesus, the Lion of Judah, the bright and morning star, the Lily of the Valley, the Rose of Sharon, the living word – Wherefore God also has greatly exalted him, giving him a name which is above every name. That at the name of Jesus every knee must bow, things in heaven, things in the earth, things under the earth. And every tongue shall confess that Jesus Christ is Lord to the glory of God the Father. Now that's authority!

Fourth, in Revelations 12, we are given the ultimate formula to overthrow our enemy. "And they overcame him (our enemy) by the blood of the lamb and by the word of their testimony and they loved not their lives unto death." Jesus is the one true savior, redeemer and deliverer of his people. He came to set the captives free, to give liberty to the bond, to heal the sick and to preach the gospel.

What I find interesting is the passage, "they did not love their lives unto death" Jesus said that, "He that finds his life shall lose it: and he that loses his life for my sake shall find it." So, it's an attitude adjustment. We must understand that we were not saved by ourselves or for ourselves. Yet too regularly, we hold onto pieces of our past lives. Why do we do this when we are promised so much more just for giving it up?

It is unfortunate that we live in fear of loosing the refuse of our lives. This is the last vantage point of "FEAR". We must remind fear that we are not buddies anymore. We must not be afraid of persecution because for Jesus sake. He prepares us that as the world hated him, it will hate us. Again, we are reminded not return evil for evil. But to bless them who curse us and pray for them who despitefully use us.

We don't have to understand the strategy of our captain; we just have to follow orders. Our captain is strong and mighty, He is faithful and is the victor. We no longer have to live behind a prison wall afraid of people or ourselves. We are given the whole kingdom of God to roam in, minister in and experience every good thing he has planned for us. But if we stand guardian over our dead body and old nature then we will not ever experience the abundant life.

Finally, about the slick, gun twirling moves as the guards leaves his post when his relief comes. Listen closely. It's summed up in two verses: Galatians 2:20, "We are crucified with Christ, nevertheless we live; yet not us; but Christ lives in us: and the life which we now live in the flesh we live by the faith of the Son of God, who loved us, and gave himself for us." And, 2 Corinthians 5:17, "Therefore if any man be in Christ, he is a new creature: old things are passed away; behold all things are become new.

We are constantly going through a changing of the guard each time we release our fears, insecurities and anxieties to the Lord. Each child he asks us to commit to him, each gift he asks us to submit to him will yield new temporary grief. Paul expresses it perfectly in his letter to the Philippians: yea doubtless, and I count all things but loss for the excellency of the knowledge of Christ Jesus my Lord: for whom I have suffered the loss of all things, and do count them but dung, that I may win Christ, and be found in him, not having mine own righteousness, which is of the law, but that which is through the faith of Christ, the righteousness which is of God by faith: that I may know him, and the power of his resurrection, and the fellowship of his sufferings, being made conformable unto his death; if by any means I might attain unto the resurrection of the dead."

Yes, we will be challenged to surrender all things to him. Why, because if we hold too tightly to the things of the world, it will hurt when he tries to pry them from our hands. We will be challenged to give up some interesting and precious things. We will have to lay them at his feet and walk away from them. We will have to walk away from the throne of grace with empty hands and hearts so that we can receive every blessed thing he has for us. All we need is an attitude adjustment and a changing of the guard. As he watches over us, we will experience the refreshing joy and sustaining peace of his pleasure.

For this lesson of Transformation we are daring to release all to God. The following questions will help us with our journey:

Read about...

- We are expected to open our hearts to give the Lord a place to rest. He will only fill those areas that we expose to him. How comfortable are you making it for him to rest? How comfortable are you making it for yourself? Can He rest if our hearts are not pure?

- The closer we get to Christ likeness, do you find that he shows you more that you must still release?

- Have you experienced the agony of having your fingers pried off of an area that God asked you to release?

- The confidence that David had in God creating and knowing everything about him incited praise and thanksgiving. What confidences were raised when he asked God about the wickedness?

- How does searching and being tried by God?

- When God exposes your wicked ways what do you do next? Do you adjust your attitude?

- Have you counted the cost of submission to God? What are the advantages and disadvantages to submission?

- Are you ready to surrender & release God?

- What key lessons have you learned from this lesson?

- Do you feel equipped to adjust your attitude after this lesson?

- How will you teach others to adjust theirs?

Let's pray.

Father God, we adore you. We are so grateful for your word. Your word that heals delivers and cleanses us. Father God, in the name of Jesus we pray that you do as only you can do. Father God we invite you into our hearts and we ask you to have your way. Shine your holy light in ever crevice and corner and crack. Show ourselves to us, Lord. For we desire to make more room for your presence to dwell. We admit continually that we still in need of a savior, healer, deliverer and redeemer.

So, in this place we exchange guards. We submit ourselves to your authority and majesty. We humbly lay down every wicked way that you expose to our minds. We no longer desire to hide the truth about ourselves from ourselves. We are thankful that you will do this for us and we will not look on as if beholding our faces in a mirror. But we will be mindful to allow the Holy Spirit to help us, teach us to eradicate all things that are against your will.

We thank you for every fortress being destroyed in Jesus name. We thank you that your perfect peace that passes all understanding will guard our hearts and minds. We thank you that this keeping peace will dwell in us and penetrate through us to those in need of peace. We thank you that you are leading us into everlasting. We honor and bless your name. Father God, we know that the good work that you have started in us; you are faithful to complete it until Jesus comes. For this, we give you praise. In the name of Jesus we pray. AMEN.

Can you see me?

"For I through the law am dead to the law,
that I might live unto God. I am crucified with Christ:
nevertheless I live; yet not I, but Christ liveth in me: and
the life which I now live in the flesh I live by the faith of
the Son of God, who loved me, and gave himself for me.
I do not frustrate the grace of God: for if righteousness
comes by the law, then Christ died in vain."
Gal. 2:19-21"

<u>Dare to be Invisible!</u>

"And be ye not conformed to this world: but be ye
transformed by the renewing of your mind, that ye may
prove what is that good, and acceptable and perfect
will of God." Romans 12:2

Last year for Christmas, we invited some friends over for Christmas brunch. After enjoying a great spread, we played a game. The game was a collection of cards with questions on them. Each person had to answer the question on the card before another card could be pulled.

The cards were biblical in nature and it was a nice gathering of Christians in the room. One of the questions read, "Which on of God's attributes would you like to have?" After a variety of answers, like, faithfulness, holiness, one person said, that they would like to be invisible. What an interesting answer. It sparked one of the most memorable conversations of my life.

It's has always intrigued me, why an awesome God want to spend time cooped up inside our limited earth-bound bodies? Why would He insist on living through us imperfect beings, to affect others, use us to fulfill His will, to represent His righteousness and to wear His name to exercise His purpose for His kingdom, when he could so easily do so without us? He loves us, that's why. He wants us to participate, cooperate and celebrate in "His Story!"

No other created being was made in His image to carry His glory, extend His grace or to fulfill His will! No, no other created being on earth, under the earth or in the heavens. He chose the form, the vessels, and the means necessary to fulfill his purposes in the earth.

As loudly as nature screams to proclaim the splendor of God, even the beauty of the seasons cannot contain His glory. The snow covered mountains we sing about as majestic, pale in comparison to His majesty.

We are that one creature created to house truth, wisdom and righteousness. Contained within us is peace that passes all understanding and unspeakable joy. We have the greatest healing power of the universe at our fingertips. Also, wonders like, grace, mercy, and compassion – we have it all. We have gifts, talents and prized skills that will make room for us. We have a mind to get wealth if we but use it for his glory. We have knowledge and understanding of mysteries. For the magnitude of the treasure we possess cannot be expressed. But the greatest of all treasure is summed up in one word, love.

A greater love than the world has ever known dwells on the inside of us. We have this treasure hid within us…but not so obscure that it cannot be seen by the spirit.

Each great example in scripture had a life-transforming encounter with the glory of God: Moses and Elijah had to hide their faces after being exposed. The priests and Levites were not able to stand and fell on their faces in worship. Isaiah had his mouth washed with a hot coal. Paul was blinded and had his sight divinely restored. John fell as a dead man and worshipped.

I am convinced that as we have our personal encounter with the Lord of Hosts that we too shall show some sign. Ah, this is the mystery? How will we display the signs of change? How will love be expressed through our fleshy filters?

Some think the signs of change are demonstrated through our attendance to Sunday and mid-week services. Some believe they are found in the songs we sing, the little dance we do, the clapping of our hands or our uplifted outstretched arms of surrender.

If it were that easy, everyone would be doing it! Some think we capture the exact instant of change, duplicate it, and package it so that next week we can come back to the same place at the same time.

We hide our love under piles of hurts, sin, shame, rejection, and indifference all week long; but think we can get it when we return week after week. We call it the glory of God. But is it really? We have become religious-junkies seeking the high of His touch that bathes us even temporarily. In great pain, we are "touched" by his healing. In sorrow, we receive a "touch" of his grace. When the storms of life are raging we get a "touch" of his peace. While in despair, we get a "touch" of his joy. These "touches" only offer temporary relief from our stresses of daily life. And can sometimes keep us from pressing on toward the real prize; possessing a heart devoted to worship.

No, the transformed soul has signs that reaches beyond the four walled structures we call churches. If we look long we can observe the signs of those transformed. It is found in how we live and interact with others. Jesus said, "on these two commandments hang all the law and the prophets; first that we love the Lord our God with all our heart, and with all our soul and with all our mind. The second is like it, that we should love our neighbor as our self." Pretty tall task if you ask me.

We love the Lord and we have the bumper stickers to prove it. But loving the Lord is not a singular activity. We must love him; allow him to love us back, so we can love his people, our neighbor.

I use to be curious about who my neighbor was until God revealed to me just how many neighbors I had. "Our neighbors are not just those in our community living on the right, left, upper and lower levels of our dwelling places. They are not limited to the family who lives across the street. Instead, the Holy Spirit revealed to me, that my community is much larger than the 2 square blocks. My neighbor includes the grocery store clerk, the mail man, the person who cut me off in traffic etc. Every person we come in contact with during our daily business becomes our neighbor. We are to love them as we love our self. Why? John said, "Herein is love, not that we loved God, but that he loved us, and sent his Son to be the propitiation for our sins. Beloved, if God so loved us, we ought also to love one another. No man hath seen God at any time. If we love one another, God dwells in us, and his love is perfected in us." (NKJV)

God longs for us to spend real quality time with Him. That He dotes over us like a hen over her chicks. He requires our slight inconvenience to approach and love on the unlovely, because they are his beloved. He also wants us to love ourselves. This is the reciprocating love affair that the God of heaven wants to have with his children. But how do we love beyond our means? Where is the source of such love? It's found in a life of worship. It is in the exchange that we find fulfillment and the strength to love beyond our means.

We will no longer tolerate temporary fixes for our "touch-addiction" when we become love agents, love conduits, and love dispensers.

God has given us love so we can love the unlovable. We are marked to appear different to those still in darkness. This uniqueness is simply the beauty of holiness given to us from a Holy God through the Holy Spirit that shines through the worshipper's heart. This is the workmanship of God manifest in our lives.

Everyone knows that you don't put your finest jewels into an ordinary box. You place them into a precious box, uniquely crafted to display the treasure. To make sure the jewels are the center of attention, the box is lined with dark velvet. In order to capture the focus of all passers by, a light is usually streaming down into the brilliance of the metal and dazzling stone. The surrounding light penetrates the stone causing the reflected rays of color to penetrate the darkest corner with shimmering fragmented lights.

Just as our heavenly Father cares for us and desires for us to reflect His love, which is the beauty of holiness. He wants to use us as boxes, to penetrate love like light rays to reach the lost, hurting and bond. The believer's heart becomes a prism and breaks the love of Christ and the love of humanity into digestible pieces for all to "taste and see that the Lord, he is good." Remember, you can't get there without worship.

He has placed his truth, word and Holy Spirit in us, "earthen vessels." Now this may come as a shock to all the "touch-junkies" but it must be said; the focus is on His word, His truth and the Holy Spirit, no on us. We are merely the jewelry boxes to carry the splendor.

So, I pose one question to you, can you see me? If you can, then I'm not invisible. I'm stealing the glory rightfully due our Father.

Jesus saith unto him, I am the way, the truth and the life: no man cometh unto the Father, but by me. If ye had known me, ye should have known my Father also: and from henceforth ye know him, and have seen him. Philip saith unto him, Lord, show us the Father, and it sufficeth us. Jesus saith unto him. Have I been so long time with you and yet hast though not known me, Philip? He that hath seen me hath seen the Father, and how sayest thou then, Show us the Father? Believest thou not that I am in the Father, and the Father in me? The words that I speak unto you I speak not of myself: but the Father that dwelleth in me, he doeth the works. Believe me that I am in the Father, and the Father in me: or else believe me for the very works' sake. (John 14:6-11).

For this lesson of Transformation: we are daring to be invisible! The following verses and questions will help us with our journey:

> Col. 3:3 "For ye are dead and your life is hid with Christ in God"

2 Cor. 4:3 "But if our gospel be hid, it is hid to them that are lost:"

Eph. 3:9 "And to make all men see what is the fellowship of the mystery, which from the beginning of the world hath been hid in God, who created all things by Jesus Christ:"

Col. 1:26 "Even the mystery which hath been hid from ages and from generations, but now is made manifest to his saints:"

Col. 2:3 "In whom are hid all the treasures of wisdom and knowledge."

Psalm 17:8 Keep me as the apple of the eye, hide me under the shadow of thy wings

- Are you visible or working on invisibility? Is your life a reflection of Jesus Christ? (Challenge: ask 3 people before the session and be honest with your answer.)

- What does a life dedicated to 24/7 worship look like? Refer to the scripture above John 14:6-14.

- Were you given grace, mercy, forgiveness, compassion and love to keep or to pass on? Are you a conduit for God or are is your plumbing clogged?

- We are to love our neighbors as ourselves, in today's society, how difficult is it to love on all that you come in contact with?

- How hard is it to love yourself? Why or why not?

- What does being invisible mean to you?

- What is the beauty of holiness and how is it demonstrated?

- What sign are you showing so all the world will know that you are "under construction for Christ"?

- What key lessons have you learned from this lesson?

- How will you become invisible (less of you and more of Christ)?

- How will you encourage others to give the glory to God?

Let's pray.

Father God, in the precious name of Jesus we pray. We come before your throne of grace seeking mercy. Mercy we ask, because until we are perfected in your love, to love as you do, walk as you do, talk as you do, we need mercy to hide the ugly in us. Father God, we know that we are created in your image and we thank you for that. So Lord, we now acknowledge that we must decrease so that you can increase in us, through us and with us. Father God, we desire to magnify your name and glorify your works in the earth. And when no one else will bless you and point the way to you for your people, use us to be the light. Yes, use us Lord as billboards to lead the lost out of bondages, to heal the sick, to extend your peace, to let your joy flow. Father God in our limited selves, we may grow tired, so we ask your forgiveness when we don't love our neighbor and even for the times when we don't love ourselves. Father God we ask you to crown us with your wisdom and understanding and knowledge to know when and to whom we must serve and lead. Father God, make us invisible so that our boastings will be of what you have done through us and for us and not of our own feeble works. Let our lives be a demonstration of your awesome power. Let even those close to us; see the change in us as we become love agents, love conduits and love dispensers. To do so, we ask only one thing, we need more of you, Gracious Father. So fill us up to the full dear

Lord of grace, fill us up with more of your love, more of your truth and more of your word. Father God, in Jesus name, we serve notice on the enemy of our soul that in and with us, the word again is made flesh; the word again is walking in the earth! Your perfect love is resting, ruling and abiding in our hearts and we are not afraid to use it! And we will be mindful to give you all the praise, glory and honor, in Jesus name. AMEN.

Let's get ready to H-U-M-B-L-E!

"And the vessel that he made of clay was marred in the hand of the potter: so he made it again another vessel, as seemed good to the potter to make it." Jer. 18:4"

Dare to be Broken!

"And be ye not conformed to this world: but be ye transformed by the renewing of your mind, that ye may prove what is that good, and acceptable and perfect will of God." Romans 12:2

Well, well, well. Congratulations! You have made it this far in your journey. You might be asking what next is required of me. We've dared to be different. We've moved forward in the transformation process and adjusted our attitudes by learning to release. We have even resigned to be invisible. Could there be more required? What more can I do to be a vessel the Lord can use? Well, the word of God says in 2 Timothy 2:21 that, If a man therefore purge himself from these, he shall be a vessel unto honor, sanctified and meet for the master's use and prepared for every good work. Oh, so this isn't about me!!!

You have probably heard the saying, "that a hard head makes for a soft backside" while you were growing up. I know my mother used to tell me that all the time. I believe she wanted me to know that stubbornness and willful living would land me on my backside on more than one occasion. She also wanted to instill in me the grace to be humble. Thanks Mom.

I am reminded that we are earthen vessels. And through life choices, we have landed on our backsides from time to time. We have been shattered and damaged from the mishandling in life. We have been dropped by family and friends. Sometimes we even mishandle ourselves. Our dreams have dried up and the residue is hard-baked under the pressure of daily living. Now what do we do? We have become untrusting, selfish, guarded, and jaded. Should we turn to yet another self-help group, look for our answer of self improvement in magazines? Sometimes even consulting with a dear friend won't bring the fulfillment we are seeking. More often than not, we, Christians, chase the conference-revival scene. Running after yet another healing, deliverance, prophesy, new word or fresh anointing.

When the running, dancing and shouting is all over, we realize that we are still left with the same cracks and caused by the stresses of life. Perhaps instead of looking to repair the cracks we should examine them for their content. After all, they are a part of us.

Upon close examination, we see that each scar is related to an incident. And each incident uncovers a precious moment in time which reminds us that we have been in a test, mess and trial. In essence, we look battle worn and headed toward total brokenness.

We shouldn't forget that each test becomes a testimony; each mess a message, and each trial results in an acquittal. The battle scars should be worn proudly because we are more than conquerors.

We should learn to "count it all joy" and say that "it was good that I was afflicted" because we know that we must join Jesus in suffering in order to really know him as the strong and mighty: deliverer, redeemer, trusted friend, and wonderful counselor.

As stated earlier, this isn't about you! It's about your witness. Funny how each fracture appearing on the surface of our earthen vessels was considered ugly scars. Yet to some, they are the most beautiful things ever seen. How is that possible?

Let's look at it objectively, shall we? If a clay pot is broken and the shards are scattered on the floor. Regardless how well we think we have picked up each fragment to reassemble the pot, we haven't. The dust remains. We can use special adhesive to hold the piece together again. We can even use sealant to fill in the cracks. But, no matter how well we force each piece together the fracture will continue to show. It is these same fractures that are vital to the beauty of the vessel.

Next, try to fill that vessel with fluid like water or oil... the life-giving water and the anointing oozes through crack, refusing to be contained. There is simply no stopping the seepage!

It will seep through the stress cracks and hairline openings, spilling onto surfaces, objects and people. Whoever handles the vessel walks away cleansed, refreshed and renewed in their spirit by the oil of gladness...? The water will refresh and the oil will stain whoever handles the object.

Even those useless vessels that we place on the shelf in the corner will be used. The seepage will collect in puddles around the base of the vessel. This puddle will affect any other object placed on the same shelf. It can even spill over on the objects on lower shelves and on to the floor and walls. Even when the vessel has long been removed, the residue will linger affecting any other objects placed on the same shelf.

This is why corporate praise and worship is so contagious. The oil of gladness fills our soul and our spirit overfills and starts to flow with praise; spilling over the brim to ignite and insight praise inside a fellow worshipper...

"my cup runneth over... Psalm 23:5

"a merry heart is good medicine" Prov.15:13,15

"joy be full" ..."joy remain" John 15:11

"Oil of joy for mourning" Isaiah 61:3

Everlasting joy shall be upon their heads Isaiah 51:11

It's no wonder why Nehemiah said that the joy of the Lord was his strength. (vs. 8:10) It is this joy that sustains us and shields us while we are going through the drama and trauma of everyday living.

But it doesn't stop there, Beloved. He also gives us His peace. Peace to be still. Being still is hard for humans but it's easy for vessels of clay. It's especially difficult for us when we are facing situations, circumstances and other issues. The very nature of situations we go through begs, no demands, for us to react. Yet in peace we can be as still as a vase, in knowing He is God, and when we will be still enough we shall see the salvation of the Lord.

And what are vessels used for anyway? In the natural, they are to carry things from one place to another; they are to contain other things. Well, it is the same in the spiritual.

We, earthen vessels, are filled with the wonderful Holy Spirit enduing us with power, love and a sound mind to exercise every good gift and to complete every good work. The Lord anoints us when he pours his oil into us. He washes

Transforming Clay into Vessels of Honor

us, with his life giving water – the word. Then he anoints us when he pours his oil of love into us. For with this love, we now are capable of loving the unlovely. We are able to minister to the hurting, confused, misguided abused and misused people of the earth.

Ah, sounds like us before we were saved, doesn't it? Yes, it does. So, we are back to the hard-head – soft bottom scenario. We have all gone through something and the key to this lesson is not to focus on all of our trial, for we are more than conquerors in Christ Jesus.

With his love he drew us to him. It is his same compassion that propels us onto the potter's wheel. And his grace that kept us there. All that we have suffered broke our hearts and humbled us to strip us of selfishness and pride. All the while being prodded, molded and fashioned in the hands of the Master Potter.

Finally, he pours into us cracked pots full of ugly scars, wounded by life in general. He pours into us like a balm and it flows from us to others.

Consider if you will this final comment; "Jesus on the night he was betrayed, took bread, gave thanks, and broke it and gave to them, saying, this is my body which is given for you, do this in remembrance of me" (Luke 22). Did you notice; after the bread of life was broken then it was given. What a blessing it is to be a blessing. But in order to do so, we must be broken first. Isaiah 53:5 so dramatically emphasizes, that "He was wounded for our transgressions, he was bruised for our iniquities: the chastisement of our peace was upon him; and with his stripes we are healed."

Consider the chastisement of our peace was upon him. Each lashing he received. Each scourging. Each and every abuse, he suffered so we could be free to come to him.

For this cause, Jesus received scars on his body, so we can be free. Free from an ordinary existence. Free from the need for acceptance. Free from fears of abandonment. We are totally free.

We are vulnerable to attacks in our body, mind and relationships. Therefore, we must gird up against the attackers within and without. These ugly scars are reminiscent of our battles with vanity, pride, and our comfort zones. These cracks etched deep within us like a road map to humility.

For this cause we are to pick up our cross and follow after him. It's no wonder we appear like sheep to the slaughter or as a peculiar people. Humility isn't as easy as it appears. Those broken vessels how have learned to submit to the gentle yet firm hand of the Father, have been empowered with grace to be and remain humble. It isn't natural to be still.

Thank you, God for allowing us to not be natural. Thank you for your super to hide our natural. Thank you for not allowing us to remain ordinary. Thank you for your extra to cover our ordinary. For this we are empowered to count it all joy! Being filled with your joy and peace, we-cracked pots are priceless! But when God puts us back together, we are completely whole, perfect and lacking nothing.

Transforming Clay into Vessels of Honor

I firmly believe that we are broken not for our own good, but for the good of others in the kingdom. Humility is our constant reminder that if not but for the grace of God, we would be consumed in our sin. We are made humble to break the hardness encasing our hearts preventing compassion and mercy from flowing in or out. God must break down this shell in order to fill us with his love so we are able to love ourselves and others. Therefore, I leave you with this to ponder, Beloved, 2 Cor. 4:7... "But we have this treasure in earthen vessels that the excellency of the power may be of God, and not of us!

For this lesson of Transformation: we are daring to be broken! The following scriptures & questions will help us with our journey:

> Ecc. 9:2... "All things come alike to all: there is one event to the righteous, and to the wicked; to the good and to the clean, and to the unclean; to him that sacrifices and to him that sacrifices not: as is the sinner; and he that swears, as he that fears an oath."

> 1 Pet. 5:10... "But the God of all grace, who hath called us unto his eternal glory by Christ Jesus, after ye have suffered a while, make you perfect, stablish, strengthen, and settle you."

2 Cor. 4:17... "For our light affliction, which is but for a moment, worketh for us a far more exceeding and eternal weight of glory;"

Rom. 5:3-5... "And not only so, but we glory in tribulation also: knowing that tribulation worketh patience: and patience, experience; and experience, hope: And hope maketh not ashamed; because the love of God is shed abroad in our hearts by the Holy Ghost which is given unto us."

James 1:2-4... "My brethren, count it all joy when you fall into divers temptations; knowing this, that the trying of your faith worketh patience. But let patience have her perfect work, that ye may be perfect and entire, wanting nothing.

Ez.11:19... "And I will give them one heart, and I will put a new spirit within you; and I will take the stony heart out of their flesh, and will give them a heart of flesh:"

Ez. 36:26... "A new heart also I will give you, and a new spirit will I put within you: and I will take away the stony heart out of your flesh, and I will give you a heart of flesh."

Ps. 119:71... "It is good for me that I was afflicted; that I might learn your statues."

Jer. 17:1 ... "The sin of Judah is written with a pen of iron, and with the point of a diamond: it is graven upon the table of your heart, and upon the horns or your altars;"

1 Cor. 2:9... "But as it is written, Eye hath not seen, nor ear heard, neither have entered into the heart of man the things which God hath prepared for them that love him."

2 Cor. 3:3... "Forasmuch as ye are manifestly declared to be the epistle of Christ ministered by us, written not with ink, but with the Spirit of the Living God; not in tablets of stone, but in the fleshy tables of the heart."

- All too often we have said that life isn't fair. Now that you are being transformed, do you still feel this way? Explain.

- Reflecting on the cracks in your life, are you able to say now that it was good that you were afflicted? Why or why not?

- What have you learned about yourself and what you have endured to this day that keeps you from falling apart completely?

- Foundations are the support of any structure, if the foundation has unrepaired cracks, what happen to the building? Relate this to your life.

- We have learned that Judah means praise, can cracks in our heart, dilute our praise? If so, can praise then act as a sealant to repair our cracks?

- As a fellow cracked pot, I've learned to let the Holy Spirit show me the areas of my life where healing is necessary and deliverance comes. Have you stopped trying to repair your own cracks?

- The hardships of life wear and tear on a person. But somehow we must still endure them. During those rough times, how has the Holy Spirit ministered to you?

- Give an example of "all things working together for good" (Romans 8:28) in your life.

- Are you all that you've been "cracked-up" to be?

- What key lessons have you learned from this lesson?

- Are you willing to let the anointing of God to flow through you?

- Can you sit back watching another brother or sister in the Lord develop their gifts?

Shall we pray?

What joy it gives us today to call you Abba Father. Yes, we call you Father because you have been more than just our Lord; you have been our Holy Father. When this world has dealt us blows and inflicted wounds, it's with a child's heart that we turn to you and you are always there. As a Father, you have nursed each wound, and tended to our needs. You have been Jehovah-Jireh our provider for each and everything in our lives. Lord God, you have even given us medicine which didn't taste good, but it was for our good. It was for our making and none of the things we endured was unto death. So, Father God we honor your word, we honor your presence and turning every situation in our lives around. We don't know how you do it. But we thank you for it. For bad things doesn't happen to good people, life does. We thank you for life. We thank you that you alone order our steps. We may not understand why we had to be divorced, bury a loved one, sickness and diseases, lack of finances to meet our daily needs, even addictions. But we still thank you for the life that we have and will no longer curse what you have blessed. And Father God, during those times of adversity Lord, when we are less trusting of you than we should, we ask your forgiveness, mercy and grace to get through them. Father God as you have shown us that the rain falls on the just and unjust alike, we allow you full reign in our lives to let our lives be a model of patience so others who are going through hard trials, will have hope. And we certainly will lead them to you with a quick and ready answer of how we made it through – for it was, is and will continue to be by your grace. We thank you for the life, ministry, and hope of Jesus. But most of all, we thank you for his resurrection. For you have shown though him, that no matter what we can endure, you will elevate us when we humble ourselves to you. So we boldly humble ourselves before you and openly make a mockery of selfishness, pride, and self-will. Demonstrate with us and through us so all the world can see that little is much in your hands. Father God, for all the broken pieces you left lying on the floor, we promise you not to revisit them again. We won't ask you for them – nor will we pick them up and try to insert them back into our lives. We thank you for a soft pliable heart. We thank you for compassion rising up in us. We thank you that joy is stronger us – for we are your children and you are our strength. We thank you for manifesting the peaceable fruit of patience in our lives. Father God we give you all praise and glory. In the precious name of Jesus we pray. AMEN

Beauty for Ashes

"Our God shall come, and shall not keep silent: a fire shall devour before him, and it shall be very tempestuous round about him. " Psalm 50:3"

Dare to be Consummed!

"And be ye not conformed to this world: but be ye transformed by the renewing of your mind, that ye may prove what is that good, and acceptable and perfect will of God." Romans 12:2

Read Isaiah 43 – 44:5

Shame on you. You mean you had no idea that all earthen wear had to go in the oven? You didn't know that all pottery had to be kilned? Really? Yes, to have a beautiful vase or yet another ceramic bowl from our children, they all must go into the furnace. The only difference is when we are placed in the furnace somebody will hear us screaming!

So, what are ashes anyway? Ashes are dead things. Dead things have no value on the open market. They can't be used to plant crops, support a building, or even to give nourishment. Spiritually speaking, ashes are the areas of our lives designated as wastes, garbage and refuse.

These remind me of several verses referring to the waste city. Picture this, the natural world as a city. This is a type of city which we bring with us as we enter into the Kingdom of God. Yet of no value or worth, we worship and praise the King of kings and Lord of lords. Everything in our lives is generally good: our health, family, friends all are in tact. We are honored by friends and foes alike. Then one day we get a whiff.

Jesus says several times, let him who has an ear to hear and eyes to see. I want to challenge you to open your nostrils and let him who has a nose to smell.

Our bodies have natural odors and although we bath in the morning, life's interactions require us to bath again. We use fragrant soaps, perfumed powders, scented oils and alcohols (cologne) to cover or mask the natural odors of our bodies. Yet the cycle continues tomorrow.

Be mindful, the same is true spiritually. We perfume our lives with praise and bath in worship and use Christendom like stick up room fresheners. Yet to no avail. Just as the natural man has an odor, the spirit-filled man is fragrant as well. We know that our prayers are in the incense in the bowls at the altar in Revelations. Yet what is that smell?

It is the stench of self and sin. It's the smell of rebellion, disobedience and unrighteousness. For this we need spiritual deodorant for those areas of our lives that we haven't submitted to our Lord.

Transforming Clay into Vessels of Honor

We conceal our holiness in bottles of unrighteousness. We powder over our sanctification with disobedience talc. We shield our consecration with Eau de toilette of rebellion. We hide our sin from everyone but God. It's no surprise that he looks at our hearts and not our actions.

Anyone who has had a biological experiment growing in their refrigerator knows this smell. Once detected it must be dealt with. We find the offence and put it in the trash.

When I was a girl, some apartment buildings had large furnaces in the basements. They carried our refuse via a shoot to the incinerator below. The fire would consume all garbage, and what was left behind was ash.

The same as with our Heavenly Father. Consider how patient God is while we struggle to be released from ungodliness, unholiness, un-righteousness and disobedience. We tend to arm wrestle with God before we yield to his promptings to take a spiritual bath. His fire not only consumes us, but purges and purifies us. It consecrates us. It sanctifies us. It makes us holy.

I used to avoid Hebrew chapter 12 for years, all because it deals with dealing with me! It speaks of chastening, love, shaking and fires. I didn't like spankings in the natural, so I didn't know what to expect in the spiritual realm.

But to my surprise it starts off by saying that we wouldn't have to be chaste if we lay aside every weight and sin that would so easily beset us and run with patience the race that is set before us. Then the word continues and warns us to not despise chastening of the Lord and faint not when (not if, but when) we are rebuked by him. Why? Because the Lord only chastens those that he loves. Do you suppose that's why our parents say, I only correct you because I love you?

Later in the same chapter we are told that this is our assurance that we are partakers of holiness. And finally, afterwards, it yields the peaceable fruit of righteousness.

Funny how if we endure the spankings, then those crooked places will be straighten out. Yet further down in the chapter, we find that God doesn't just stop there. He will also stand as our judge in all of heaven. "Whose voice then shook the earth: but now he hath promised, saying Yet once more I shake not the earth only but also heaven. And this word, yet once more signified the removing of those things made and those things which cannot be shaken may remain" ... "For our God is a consuming fire." (vs. 26-27, 29).

As children of God we must be taught, nurtured and yes disciplined. Taught lessons of trust, virtue, and temperance aren't easy. We are naturally control freaks and suspicious. But learning self-control and trusting in God will lead to a life of purity never before experienced.

While God chastens those he loves – some days I feel extra special! We can't despise being chaste because if we are to be found "like Him" then we have to separate ourselves from any and every ungodly thing, act, thought and person.

Don't get me wrong. Sometimes I didn't yield to the Holy Spirit's guidance and teachings and was found on several occasions with my hand in the fire still clutching the very thing he asked me freely to give. There are times even when the fire has to pry the old nature out of my heart. Then I remember if God doesn't want me to have it, then I shouldn't want it either. I can feel the grasp ease slightly with each thought, until finally God blows on the ashes in my mind and I can see the beauty that remains. .

So, chastening correcting and the blazing heat of the refiners fire is not for naught. Nope, it isn't. So, what is it good for, you ask? Glad you asked. I love the Old Testament. I believe it has some of the most poetic verses in scripture. But it also introduces us to the character of God as well as laying the foundation of the relationship God desires with his people.

Proverbs contains an example of our nature, saying that if we don't control ourselves, we will be as a city without walls. Interesting concept isn't it? In ancient times a city without walls was unprotected, easily overrun by predators, man and beast, alike. That's nothing I would want to live through. How about you?

The walls are the most interesting analogy. In Exodus, the Hebrews were charged to make bricks without straw. To the Egyptians surprise, they did it. Yet, while they made the bricks without straw – the bricks still needed to be baked in order to harden and set.

I find this interesting because later in the New Testament, we are called "lively stones" by Peter. The stubble and straw is all consumed in God's refining fire. So, collectively let's heave into the fire, the lust of the flesh, lust of the eyes, pride of life, bitterness, filthy communication, wrath, anger, clamor and evil speaking, malice.

In closing, as we dare to be consumed God's holy fire, we will only make more room for his beauty: more room for love; more room for grace, and more room for compassion and more room for his righteousness. How so? He will blow the ash out of the way and our stock will increase. For in Him and in Him only is our ability to love even the unlovely. For in Him and in Him only will we be grace-full. In Him and in Him only is compassion found and dispensed according to His will. In Him and in Him only is our hope of righteousness.

We will be left with something much more valuable than the treasures of earthly wealth. These treasures we hold in earthen vessels which have been purged and purified like silver and gold. Who could dispute the captivating mystery of unconditional love, unmerited grace, pure selfless compassion and spirit fortifying righteousness of Jesus? This beauty shines more brilliant than polished silver or gold?

We find throughout scripture that God has a marketplace where his currency of exchange is grace, when we bring our faith to the teller window. As our faith increases, we yield more easily to him. He extends his grace until we surrender to him. It's like credit! He said that he would give us beauty for ashes, and He is faithful to His promises. Hmmmm, we smell better already: guess we took the trash out!

For this lesson of Transformation: we are daring to be consumed! The following scriptures & questions will help us with our journey.

> Prov. 25:28... "He that hath no rule over his own spirit is like a city that is broken down, and without walls."

> Romans 8: 4... "That the righteousness of the law might be fulfilled in us, who walk not after the flesh, but after the Spirit."

> Gal. 5:16-17, 25... "This I say, Walk in the Spirit, and ye shall not fulfill the lust of the flesh. For the flesh lusted against the Spirit, and the Spirit against the flesh: and these are contrary the one to the other: so that ye cannot do the things that ye would." ... "If we live in the Spirit, let us also walk in the Spirit."

> Ez. 36:27... "And I will put my spirit within you, and cause you to walk in my statues, and ye shall keep my judgments, and do them."

> Eph. 2:15-22... "Having abolished in his flesh the enmity, even the law of commandments contained

in ordinances; for to make himself twain one new man, so making peace: And that he might reconcile both unto God in one body by the cross, having slain the enmity thereby: And came and preached peace to you which were afar off, and to them that were nigh. For through him we both have access by one Spirit unto the Father. Now therefore ye are no more strangers and foreigners, but fellow citizens with the saints, and of the household of God; and are built upon the foundation of the apostles and prophets, Jesus Christ, himself being the chief corner stone; In whom all the building fitly framed together growth unto an holy temple in the Lord: in whom ye also are builded together an habitation of God through the Spirit."

1 Peter 2:5... "Ye also, as lively stones, are built up a spiritual house, an holy priesthood, to offer up sacrifices, acceptable to God by Jesus Christ."

Hebrews 12:26-29... "Whose voice then shook the earth: but now he hath promised, saying, Yet once more I shake not the earth only, but also heaven. And this word, yet once more, signified the removing of those things which cannot be shaken may remain. Wherefore we receive a kingdom which cannot be moved, let us have grace, whereby we may serve

God acceptable with reverence and godly fear: For our God is a consuming fire."

- One of God's promises is that He will never leave you nor forsake you. Jesus even said, "That he is with us always." Are you comforted knowing this is the relationship He desires to have with you?

- How is this relationship reflected in your life?

- When God knocks on the door of our hearts longing to come in and sup with us, is he treated as an invited guest – full of formality or as a close friend?

- Having made room in our heart to receive the Lord's fullness, we are to give Him full reign of our house or we sometimes leave him to only go as far as the living room, bathroom and dining room? Or do you allow him to open your refrigerator to see your leftovers, look into your cupboards, closets, under the bed and in the medicine chest?

- Are you offended when (not if) He does this?

- Our friendship-relationship with the Lord develops it stages through prayer. Have you noticed your prayer life changing from simply asking: "give me, get me, loan me, and let me have" to asking him only one question – how may I better serve you?

- What has this transition done for you?

- Friends pick up traits and habits of each other. Reflecting on the beauty of the Lord's character, can you recognize a difference in your own? Are you looking more like him, day by day?

- Speaking of the Lord's character, what are the most beautiful characteristics or attributes of the Lord to you? Explain please.

- Which characteristics or attributes have not been matured in your life yet?

- How will these characteristics or attributes be matured in you?

- What key lessons have you learned from this lesson?

- How will you apply it to your life?

- How will you teach others?

All minds clear and hearts open. Let's pray?

Oh precious Lord, we are so honored today to be able to call you our friend. What joy it gives us to know that you are a friend who sticks closer than any brother. Lord God, we know lord that you are a promise keeper. As you have promised that you would not leave us comfortless but would send comforter. We thank you for the comfort of the Holy Spirit today. Father God, we thank you for Jesus Christ today. For through his life, we have a model of your beauty and your desire for how we should live. Through his death, you taught us to lay down our very own agenda for the sake of love. Through his burial, you have taught us the value of righteousness being found only in him and not in ourselves. By His rising from the grave, you have taught us victory to overcome every weight that would beset us. And by his ascension to the throne beside you Father, you have taught us how to serve you – to the full and complete measure. Father God, it brings such peace to our hearts know that we have nothing to be ashamed of, nothing to fear, and nothing to hold us from allowing your full measure to flow through our lives. We declare you sovereign to your word and your plan. We proclaim you beautiful. We pronounce you a righteous judge. And we decree you as our forgiving Lord. We will praise you for your grace and mercy. You are so patient us. You encourage us to be go through the fire and be transformed, run the race, fight the good fight and to be transformed, to put of the old man and put on the new, be strengthened in the inner man – so that we have strength to endure, so that we may be city-lights to lead other out of darkness of the wilderness and into the light of your dear son. You have set us up in high esteem and we bless your name as your Beloved. Because of your faith in us Lord, we will do all we can to serve you, represent your kingdom as righteous ambassadors. For all that you have done and all that you will do, we give you praise, glory and honor, in the name of Jesus. AMEN

The Potter & the clay

"Jeremiah. 18:1-15 "

Dare to be Clay!

"And be ye not conformed to this world: but be ye transformed by the renewing of your mind, that ye may prove what is that good, and acceptable and perfect will of God." Romans 12:2

All of us are in various stages in our lives. Some are in a stage of usefulness, some waiting to be used and others just being formed for future use. Regardless of the stages we are currently in, we all start out the same. We will ask the same questions. Who am I? Why am I here? What is my purpose? Is this the best it will ever be?

No matter our backgrounds, these questions of life started each of us on a quest. Hurdling socio-economic status, gender, ethnicity, and nationality we were all on a quest. The quest of our self-discovery.

Transforming Clay into Vessels of Honor

Isaiah 64:8 declares that God is the potter and we are the clay. Jeremiah continues this theme in chapter 18:2-6, where we find an interesting passage of a potter working a work on a wheel. The work was marred in the hands of the potter's hands so he made a new vessel. Surprisingly, it was good to the potter to make it.

For years, I've read these verses and became giddy from the possibilities of who I would was, not who I would become. My parents instilled in me the notion that I could be anything I wanted to be. I'm sure you were told the same from someone in your lifetime.

These possibilities sometimes altered our life choices by seeking to perform to the standards of men. As a result, we're all left with a void that could not be filled. That is to say, it could not be filled by any relationship, political affiliation, organization, social clubs, sports activities, education or vocation. It couldn't even be filled with conventional religion.

As the hole in our hearts grew wider and deeper, we discovered that our self-discovery doesn't answer the question, it only prompts more questions. So my friend, where are we to go to elevate the ache inside? What can we find to fill the void in the middle of our hearts?

Paul expounds in answer to this question. In Romans 9:21, we find that the potter has power over the clay; even choosing some to become vessels of honor and some unto dishonor, some as vessels of wrath and vessels of mercy.

This was always a mystery to me. I always viewed it as selection of one person over another to be honorable or not. This didn't sound like the gracious God who wished that none would perish. However,

inspecting the verse to uncover the mystery within we find fur little words..."of the same lump". We all have areas of virtues and shortcomings. As a result, we must turn our minds and hearts to our Creator God for the answer to the ultimate questions, who am I? Why did you make me? Is this the best it will ever be?

Yes, turning back to God will answer these questions and offer us hope for a future. After all, he made us; surely he would know the purpose. He would know how to sustain us. Through eternity, He has waited like a Father for his prodigal children to return. Upon arrival, we find ourselves in the tender hands of the potter, riding His wheel of life, being transformed into the perfect image of his son, Jesus.

He turns our cold, self-deceiving hearts of stone into pliable soil ready for good seeds. He expects to see and encourages us to be fruitful and yield a harvest. A harvest of the finest fruits, so the world can take a bite, taste and see that the Lord is good.

It's not an overnight sensation or a hit and miss happenchance. It's brought about only by the protective guidance of calculated grace. I used the term calculated because we are told that each of us is fearfully and wonderfully made. Each of us is on his mind from eternity. He knew us before he formed us. This tells me that He, who made the beginning and the ending, was thinking of us when he created anything.

He placed the earth, hung it on nothingness, in the exact location to maintain a temperature which would be compatible with our existence. The slightest tittles in any direction would send the earth into extremes of being too hot or too cold to maintain life as we know it.

But he didn't stop there. He provided food and water before he made mankind. Even after, His provision doesn't stop there. He placed different gifts, talents and skills inside each of us. Why? So we could used these gifts, talents and skills develop technological inventions, establish relationships, and still come up feeling empty. God forbid. So why do we have these gift then? To give us an expected end.

Remember, the potter has power over the clay. The expected end is that we come back to him. His word declares that, nothing shall overtake us that us not common to man, but he will make a way of escape for us. Ah-ha, enters Jesus Christ, our escape clause. Until we discover the magnitude of grace through faith, that Jesus Christ is the embodiment of pure love, we will remain empty vessels and our end will not be at the point of the perfect plan God had for our lives. Without the love of Jesus and grace we will remain unfulfilled, dark and perverse. We would be locked inside our fleshy selves unable to life fruitful lives.

From time to time, we end our ride on the wheel to sit on the shelf. Again a period of calculated grace to fortify us with yet a deeper need. These are the moments in our lives when after knowing his touch, loving kindness we might feel dry, barren and alone. While being fashioned wasn't joyous, we long for the nearness of his fellowship as his tender hands molded us. His tender hands made it a pleasure to suffer through.

No one likes the shelf sitting stage either. We murmur and complain about not being useful. We feel as though we aren't doing anything. But it is so necessary to establish us, settle us, perfect us, so that the only want we have is that of wanting God's nearness again.

This is the period where we feel like we are waiting on God to move on our behalf. We have prayed and prayed and prayed. Ah, yes, after having done all, we must continue to stand and stand therefore. This is the period when all that we had been given freely must be worked out through our skin. This is the period when the seeds become active and the branches are full with blooms and immature fruit. Thank God for the grace to have us wait this period of time out sitting on the shelf. Yes, be joyful Beloved, because immature fruit has no sweetness or goodness in it.

Soon enough when the season has come and the fruit is mature, we will eventually hear Him whisper, "Go!" Go where? Go and do what? How can I go, I'm just a vessel full of imperfections? Again, He'll whisper, "Trust me and go!"

We had no clue that the shelf was a display case for prized possessions. They look beautiful in the case, but to really show them off, one must open the case and let the on-looker touch the vessel.

He was pouring into us the wisdom and knowledge to reveal the mysteries of grace. So we would be equipped to go!

We earthen vessels have no value on the open market of life. But in the spiritual realm, we have hidden treasures inside. The Holy Spirit will minister through us. Its then we find out where we are to go and what we are to do. He sends us out into the world as priceless vessels meet for the Master's use.

He sends us to the lost broken hearted, to the captives, to those needing healing, and deliverance. He sends us to a crooked and perverse nation where we will shine as lights. Like a city of lights on a hill or a lighthouse by the sea. Both are inviting beacons of hope for the weary traveler lost in the wilderness or lost at sea. They not only inspire comfort and rest, but they also point out traps and snares on land and the dangerous rocks at sea.

So, fellow clay mates, climb aboard the potter's wheel and really discover who you were created to be. Then wait on the shelf while being filled with his glory, grace and wisdom. So when you are called out to go, you will be blameless and harmless in the midst of a crooked and perverse nation among whom you shine as light to the world.

For this lesson of Transformation: we are daring to be clay! The following scriptures & questions will help us with our journey:

> Prov. 25:28... "He that hath no rule over his own spirit is like a city that is broken down, and without walls."

> Romans 8: 4... "That the righteousness of the law might be fulfilled in us, who walk not after the flesh, but after the Spirit."

> Gal. 5:16-17, 25... "This I say, Walk in the Spirit, and ye shall not fulfill the lust of the flesh. For the flesh lusted against the Spirit, and the Spirit against the flesh: and these are contrary the one to the other: so that ye cannot do the things that ye would." ... "If we live in the Spirit, let us also walk in the Spirit."

> Ez. 36:27... "And I will put my spirit within you, and cause you to walk in my statues, and ye shall keep my judgments, and do them."

> Eph. 2:15-22... "Having abolished in his flesh the enmity, even the law of commandments contained in ordinances; for to make himself twain one new man, so making peace: And that he might reconcile

both unto God in one body by the cross, having slain the enmity thereby: And came and preached peace to you which were afar off, and to them that were nigh. For through him we both have access by one Spirit unto the Father. Now therefore ye are no more strangers and foreigners, but fellow citizens with the saints, and of the household of God; and are built upon the foundation of the apostles and prophets, Jesus Christ, himself being the chief corner stone; In whom all the building fitly framed together growth unto an holy temple in the Lord: in whom ye also are builded together an habitation of God through the Spirit."

1 Peter 2:5... "Ye also, as lively stones, are built up a spiritual house, an holy priesthood, to offer up sacrifices, acceptable to God by Jesus Christ."

Hebrews 12:26-29... "Whose voice then shook the earth: but now he hath promised, saying, Yet once more I shake not the earth only, but also heaven. And this word, yet once more, signified the removing of those things which cannot be shaken may remain. Wherefore we receive a kingdom which cannot be moved, let us have grace, whereby we may serve God acceptable with reverence and godly fear: For our God is a consuming fire."

- One of God's promises is that He will never leave you nor forsake you. Jesus even said, "That he is with us always." Are you comforted knowing this is the relationship He desires to have with you?

- How is this relationship reflected in your life?

- When God knocks on the door of our hearts longing to come in and sup with us, is he treated as an invited guest – full of formality or as a close friend?

- Having made room in our heart to receive the Lord's fullness, we are to give Him full reign of our house or we sometimes leave him to only go as far as the living room, bathroom and dining room? Or do you allow him to open your refrigerator to see your leftovers, look into your cupboards, closets, under the bed and in the medicine chest?

- Are you offended when (not if) He does this?

- Our friendship-relationship with the Lord develops it stages through prayer. Have you noticed your prayer life changing from simply asking: "give me, get me, loan me, and let me have" to asking him only one question – how may I better serve you?

Transforming Clay into Vessels of Honor

- What has this transition done for you?

- Friends pick up traits and habits of each other. Reflecting on the beauty of the Lord's character, can you recognize a difference in your own? Are you looking more like him, day by day?

- Speaking of the Lord's character, what are the most beautiful characteristics or attributes of the Lord to you? Explain please.

- Which characteristics or attributes have not been matured in your life yet?

- How will these characteristics or attributes be matured in you?

- What key lessons have you learned from this lesson?

- How will you remember that you are only clay?

- How will you teach others?

Let's go to our Father

What joy it is Lord God to know that you are the one who sits on the throne of grace, you are the one who gives us good gifts, you are the one who thinks about us and wants to be with us more than we do sometimes. Oh Lord that you would forgive us for those times when we neglect to honor you with your time and money and friendship. Because Lord you have shown us the more excellent way, we desire to follow. We ask Lord that you would help us to be like clay – stay where we are put, that we don't rebel against you, complain and murmur. Oh Lord that we would learn how to be still. Father be patient with us. and impart unto us, a heart to dwell in your presence with knowledge that your way is right, true and will give us much success. Thank you Lord. In the name of your Son, Jesus. AMEN

Fit for the Master's use

Gal. 4:19, My little children, of whom I travail in birth again until Christ be formed in you

Dare to be Vessels of Honor

"And be ye not conformed to this world: but be ye transformed by the renewing of your mind, that ye may prove what is that good, and acceptable and perfect will of God." Romans 12:2

Finally, we have a grasp of how we are transformed from clay into vessels of honor. This begs the question of when? We've been on the potter's wheel, going round and round. We have been shaped, molded folded, fashioned and poked. We've been put in the fire to test that His form would hold. There are even times when we're brought back to the wheel for more add-ons and subtractions. We have been washed, and put on shelves for display. We have even been used to some extent. Some of us have been polished, glazed, and painted. Yet, we still have the question of arrival? Completion? Finality?

To tell you that there was an end to the process would be telling you a lie. There is no conclusion. Yet, we can be in our purpose, our destiny and feel fulfilled. So to identify the moment we became a vessel of honor, we must first separate the making process from the creating process.

Isaiah had something to say about this. In chapter 49:5, the Lord says, "And now, saith the Lord that formed me from the womb to be his servant, to bring Jacob again to him, Though Israel be not gathered, yet shall I be glorious in the eyes of the Lord, and my God shall be my strength.

Gal. 4:19, My little children, of whom I travail in birth again until Christ be formed in you,... Jer. 1:5 Before I formed thee in the belly I knew thee; and before thou camest forth out of the womb I sanctified thee, and I ordained thee a prophet unto the nations.

We are informed in Jeremiah that God knew us while we were still in our mother's womb. Solomon spoke of being shaped in Proverbs 4:23 "Keep thy heart with all diligence; for out of it are the issues of life. Put away from thee a forward mouth and perverse lips put far from thee. Let thine eyes look right on and be thine eyelids look straight before thee. Ponder the path of thy feet, and let all thy ways be established. Turn not to the right hand nor to the left: remove thy foot from evil."

Have you ever gazed into the eyes of your child, spouse, parent or friend? If you look closely very closely you will see the same image in each. You peer into the face and suddenly the face disappears. The image in the eye captivates you, holding you transfixed. When suddenly you realize that the image is your own reflection.

You're a vessel of honor when you look so long into the man of Jesus that your heart melts, and you desire only what he desires for you. You're a vessel of honor when you gaze into the eyes of your Beloved and risk seeing yourself as you really are…you're a vessel of honor when you can see your own image peeking back at you only this time, something is different. He allows you to see yourself as he sees you.

This vision of "the you", royal, yet peculiar, holy, righteous, sanctified able of great exploits, signs, miracles and wonders. This image He showed you. This wonderful vision of the new you is not quiet so new. It's the image of your Beloved peering back at you.

Moses is my fondest example of seeking to understand this Holy God who had called him to come up on the mountain. Recall in Exodus when he asked God to show him His glory? God told him, he wouldn't be able to see His face and live, but he would have his "goodness" to go pass him, show him His hind parts and proclaim His name before Him. Remember what happened next? God put him in the cleft of a rock (The Rock for his safekeeping – the Rock, Jesus). Then God put his hand over him (the blessings, covering, hedge, guidance, comforting – the Holy Spirit).

Then God descended in the cloud, and stood with him there, and proclaimed the name of the Lord. And the Lord passed by before him, and proclaimed, the Lord, The Lord God, merciful and gracious, longsuffering and abundant in goodness and truth, Keeping mercy for thousands, forgiving iniquity and transgression and sin, and that will by no means clear the guilty; visiting the iniquity of the fathers upon the children and upon the children's children, unto the third and to the forth generation. And Moses made haste, and bowed his head toward the earth and worshipped." (Ex. 34:5-8).

The beauty of this passage is how God revealed every action He made to Moses. Also how God unveiled His word to Moses. God showed Moses everything in Genesis.

I always wondered in those 40 years of wandering, when did Moses have time to write the first book? When did he and God sit down and discuss creation? God, who in a few seemingly non-imposing verses reveals his promises, faithfulness, perfect plan for humanity and even the prophecy of Jesus Christ (see Gen. 3:15). He explained the framework and intent for creation. This was the hind parts that God showed Moses on the mountain.

So with this understanding we return to the similarity between the potter's wheel and the potter and the clay, all being revealed in Genesis chapter one, verses 1 and 2.

God in the beginning created... the earth was without form.... And the potter works a work on a wheel.. it seemed marred in the hands of the potter... back on the wheel and create a vessel, as it was good for the potter to make it.

Transforming Clay into Vessels of Honor

You're a vessel of honor when you realize that you are in the potter's hands and it was good for the potter to make you.

For this lesson of Transformation: we are daring to be vessels of honor! The following scriptures & questions will help us with our journey:

> 2 Cor. 3:18... "But we all, with open face beholding as in a glass the glory of the Lord, are changed into the same image from glory to glory, even as by the Spirit of the Lord"

> Matt. 16:13-16... "When Jesus came into the coasts of Caesarea Philippi, he asked his disciples, saying, Whom do men say that I the Son of man am? And they said, Some say that thou art John the Baptist: some, Elias; and others, Jeremias, or one of the prophets. He saith unto them, But whom say ye that I am? And Simon Peter answered and said, Thou art the Christ, the Son of the Living God."

> Isaiah 64:8... "But now, O Lord, thou art our Father; and we are the clay, and thou our potter; and we all are the work of thy hand."

> Jeremiah 18:4,6... "And the vessel that he made of clay was marred in the hand of the potter: so he made it again another vessel, as seemed good to the potter

to make it. .... O house of Israel, cannot I do with you as this potter? Saith the Lord. Behold, as the clay is in the potter's hand, so are ye in mine hand, O house of Israel.

Romans 9:20-21... Nay but, O man, who art thou that repliest against God? Shall the thing formed say to him that formed [it], Why hast thou made me thus? Hath not the potter power over the clay, of the same lump to make one vessel unto honor, and another unto dishonor?

Eph. 2:20... "For we are the workmanship, created in Christ Jesus unto good works, which God hath before ordained that we should walk in them.

- Do you feel equipped to adjust your attitude after this lesson?

- What key lessons have you learned from this lesson?

- How will you help others to adjust theirs?

Let us pray.
    Dear Lord and the source of our hope. May we be found unmovable, unshakable, always abounding in the work of crucifying your flesh so that your inner man is strength-

ened. Oh Father, that we may flourish as a beautiful flower before the Lord as you feast with Him daily. You love us so completely and perfectly. There is none like you. You have removed the desolate places and waste lands when you took our stony hearts and given us hearts of flesh. You have given us hearts to seek you, to know you and to desire you. But mostly Lord, you have given us your testimony as witnesses in this earth that You reign supreme. Father we couldn't thank you enough for your Son. We only ask that you minister to us when we hedge your greatness with fears and doubts. Thank you for this love affair Lord Jesus. In your matchless and mighty name we pray. AMEN.

Conclusion

I want to thank you for taking this journey with me. I pray it is the first of many that you and I will share. Mind you, this is not to be considered an exhaustive, all inclusive work. Instead, it is a prelude to a series of like minded books, to perfect the saints. We all must be about our Father's business.

It is my hearts desire as you've journeyed through these pages that you willingly purposefully sought out a deeper relationship with our heavenly Father. Be warned, as you approach pure Holiness, that much will be revealed to you about you. Yes, approach with caution. For in doing so, you will be changed. If Jesus did anything for us, besides opening the portal of heaven for us, it was to bring us to the Throne of Grace. Where seated in majesty, splendor, wonder, excellence, judging rightly, merciful, and the fullness of truth is our Father God.

Yes, Jesus is coming for a bride, who will reign with Him for an eternity; Where together they may worship the Father, in Spirit and Truth. She will walk in the grace and splendor of her Bridegroom. For he will bestowed upon her many crowns and adorned her with His glory. Even now, she groans with all creation for her Bridegroom, to continue perfecting her, at all cost. To purge out all iniquity, transgression, and evil work so that she is without spot or blemish. She cries with the Spirit, "Come! Bring your purging fire. Come! Bring your hyssop. Come! Bring your looking glass and search me and know me. Come!"

This high cost of holiness, godliness and purity comes with a high price. Just read Isaiah 53 sometimes, for understanding. To know that our Bridegroom has suffered so much just to have us, shouldn't we also join Him in that suffering? As he pants waiting for the fullness of time before His return, should we?

Be encouraged, my friends God has great things planned for you. The perfecting of your faith and bringing forth the beauty of holiness in you, is His goal. Notice, I have not told you that it would be easy. In fact, it's not for the faint hearted. Some will opt to receive grace unto salvation while others will long to walk the corridors of our heavenly mansion, peering into each room. However, He will finish the good work He's started in you. That good work, is bringing you into the fullness of His dearly Beloved Son, till He be made manifested in you.

You shall see when you hand over more and more to Him, he will reveal the mystery of His desire for you. And you will most assuredly hear Him say, "I am my Beloved's and my Beloved is mine. He feeds his flock among the lilies. He is the Lily in the Valley and how beautiful they are when displayed in vessels of honor.

My friends, I can't think of anyone more precious than you, and I can't think of anyone more lovely than Jesus. He is my Beloved, and He is my friend. Can't you just hear Him saying, "Come away My Beloved, come away"? Join Him in a dance of intimacy as you live out each day of the life He has planned for you. Lean on Him, trust in Him, move where He moves, step where He steps. And you will hear a faint whisper in the wind saying, "Who is this coming up out of the wilderness leaning on the arm of their Beloved"? Yes they will notice a change in you as you've been and will continue to be transformed by the Master Potter.

It is my honor to pray for you (and myself) in this closing prayer.

Father, I come to your throne of grace in the name of Your Son in the power of Your Holy Spirit, on behalf of my friends, your sons and daughters. I lift them to your throne of grace today. It is for this cause I bow my knees unto the Father of our Lord Jesus Christ, of whom the whole family in heaven and earth is named, that He would grant you according to the riches of His glory, to be strengthened with might by His Spirit in the inner man; that Christ may dwell in our hearts by faith; that we, being rooted and grounded in love, may be able to comprehend with all saints what is the breadth, and length, and depth and height; and to know the love of Christ, which passes knowledge, that we might be filled with all the fullness of God.

Now unto Him that is able to do exceeding abundantly above all that we ask or think, according to the power that works in us, unto Him be glory in the church by Christ Jesus throughout all ages, world without end.

Father, I thank you for my sisters and brothers that I mention in this prayer. I ask you Lord to give us the spirit of wisdom and revelation in the knowledge of Him: the eyes of our understanding being enlightened; that we may know what is the hope of His calling, and what the riches of the glory of his inheritance in the saints, and what is the exceeding greatness of His power toward us who believe, according to the working of His mighty power, which He wrought in Christ, when he raised him from the dead, and set Him at His own right hand in the heavenly places, far above all principalities, and powers, and might, and dominion, and every name that is named, not only in this world, but also in that which is to come: and hath put all things under His feet, and gave Him to be the head over all things to the church, which is His body, the fullness of Him that fills all in all.

Father, that we will be strong in the Lord, and in the power of His might. That we will put on the whole armour of God, that we may be able to stand against the wiles of the devil. For we wrestle not against flesh and blood, but against principalities, against powers, against the rulers of the darkness of this world, against wickedness in high places. Wherefore Father, that we would take up the whole armour of God, that we may be able to withstand in the evil day, and having done all, to stand. Stand therefore, having our loins girt about with truth, and having on the breastplate of rightousness; and our feet shod with the preparation of the gospel of peace; above all, taking the shield of faith, where we shall be able to quench the fiery darts of the wicked. And that we take the helmet of salvation, and the sword of the Spirit, which is the word of God: Praying always with all prayer and supplication in the Spirit, and watching thereunto with all perseverance and supplication for all saints; and for us, that utterance may be given unto us, that we may open our mouths boldly, to make known the mystery of the gospel.

For though we walk in the flesh, we do not war after the flesh: (For the weapons of our warfare are not carnal, but might through God to the pulling down of strong holds; Casting down imaginations, and every high thing that exalts itself against the knowledge of God, and bringing into captivity every thought to the obedience of Christ; And having a readiness to revenge all disobedience, when their obedience is fulfilled.

Finally Father that we work out our own salvation in fear and trembling. That we may be blameless and harmless as sons and daughters of God, without rebuke, in the midst of a crooked and perverse nation, among whom we shine as lights.

Father that we are careful for nothing; but in everything by prayer and supplication with thanksgiving we will let our requests be made known unto You. That your peace O God, which passes all understanding, shall keep our heart and mind through Christ Jesus.

I pray that we be likeminded with Christ and be able to think on those things which are true, honest, just, pure, lovely, of good report, and if there be any virtue and praise, let us think on those things and allow it to be manifest through us so that your peace Father will keep us. Father I will await the praise reports of the glorious things You have done for us and together we shall be mindful to give You all thanksgiving, praise, glory and honor. In the matchless name above all names, Your Son, Jesus, I pray.
Amen.

ACKNOWLEDGEMENTS

I have dedicated this book to all who encouraged me. But now, I'd like to put a face on three special women, who have always been instrumental to this work. You have each ministered to me in grace, love and always with exceeding joy; even when I was less than joyful. You have encouraged me, nudged me, and you unceasingly prayed for me. So I give you each a heartfelt "Thank you and Atta-girl" to my sisters: Mrs. Selma Cordell, Ms. Eugenia Glasco, and Mrs. Wanda Harney. Had it not been for your encouragement, I would have never sat down and asked the Lord what would he have me to do. Thank you each for your laughter, tears, prayers and rebukes. You are Vessels of Honor, and don't let anyone ever tell you different! The Lord God bless you, keep you, return back to you a hundred-fold what you have poured into me. I love you ladies. Yo' Sistah, Maria!

C. S. Lewis
Donna Partow – "Becoming a vessel of honor"
King James Version – Spirit Filled Bible
The Message Bible
New King James Version - John MacArthur Study Bible
Strong's Concordance
www.blueletterbible.com
www.settingcaptivesfree.com
www.studylight.com
Explore the Book

RECOMMENDED READING LIST

Gene Edwards
"Secrets to the Christian Life",
"The Divine Romance",
"The Day I was Crucified."

Bruce Wilkerson
"Prayer of Jabez",
"Secrets of the Vine"

John Piper
"Desiring God",
"The Passion of Christ"

Wesley and Stacy Campbell,
"Praying the Bible"

Cynthia Heald,
"A Woman's Journey to the Heart of God"

Hannah Hubbard,
"Hind's feet in High Places"

Max Lacado
"No Wonder We Call Him Savior"

Frances Frangipane
"Stronghold of God",
"Holiness, Truth and the Presence of God"

Felicia Pickett,
"Presenting the Holy Spirit",
"Stones of Rememberance",
"Possessing the Promise Land",
"Five Laws of the Dying Seed"

S. J. Hill, "Burning Desire"

Author's Bio

Maria Rice is proud to be counted worthy that Jesus Christ died for her, so that she could join Him as her beloved bridegroom. Supported by her husband, family, and friends, acquired her B.A. in Biblical Counseling and is now pursuing her graduate degree with certification in Sexual Addictions from Master's Divinity School.

She is also founder of Genesthai Ministries. Genesthai Ministries provides alternative counseling services in the area of life-skills coaching, lay-Biblical Counseling, mentorship programs and offer bible studies, training and equipping the saints of God. She is a bible study facilitator for women in a dual facility: those in a judicial drug rehabilitation program and those in transitional housing after being released from state prison.

Having a passion to see all set free of the weight and sin bondages that would so easily beset them, she is also a mentor with www.settingcaptivesfree.com.

By the time this work is complete she will plunge into the next books of the "Grow in Faith and Godliness Series". Look for her next books in the series: "Ruined by Grace", "So, This Is How We Die", and "In His Image", to be released soon.

In all this, nothing is to be compared to her relationship with the Holy Trinity, Father, Son and Holy Spirit. Her only request is that you falling in love with Him too. Keep her in your prayers.

Printed in the United States
58687LVS00002B/36